Rhythm & Booze

Rhythm & Booze

POEMS BY JULIE KANE

University of Illinois Press

Urbana and Chicago

♾ This book is printed on acid-free paper.

Library of Congress Cataloging-in-Publication Data
Kane, Julie.
Rhythm & booze : poems / by Julie Kane.
p.   cm. — (The national poetry series)
ISBN 0-252-02865-1 (cloth : alk. paper)
ISBN 0-252-07140-9 (pbk. : alk. paper)
I. Title.
II. Series.
PS3611.A763R48   2003
811'.54—dc21   2002155959

THE NATIONAL POETRY SERIES

The National Poetry Series was established in 1978 to ensure the publication of five poetry books annually through participating publishers. Publication is funded by the late James A. Michener, the Copernicus Society of America, Edward J. Piszek, the Lannan Foundation, the National Endowment for the Arts, and the Tiny Tiger Foundation.

2002 Competition Winners

Julie Kane of Natchitoches, Louisiana, *Rhythm & Booze*
Chosen by Maxine Kumin; published by the University of Illinois Press

William Keckler of Harrisburg, Pennsylvania, *Sanskrit of the Body*
Chosen by Mary Oliver; published by Viking Penguin

Elenai Sikelianos of Boulder, Colorado, *Footnotes to the Lambs*
Chosen by Diane Ward; published by Green Integer

Gabriel Spera of Los Angeles, California, *The Standing Wave*
Chosen by Dave Smith; published by HarperCollins

Meredith Stricker of Carmel, California, *Tenderness Shore*
Chosen by Fred Chappell; published by Louisiana State University Press

Acknowledgments

The author thanks the editors of the following publications in which these poems first appeared:

Able Muse: "Thoughtball Villanelle"

The Bartender Poems (ed. Geoffrey Godbert [London: Greville Press, 1991]): "Kissing the Bartender," "Bar Noise," "Angel of Bars and Nightclubs," and "The Bartender Quits Drinking"

Crescent: The Journal of Public Affairs and Urban Life: "Maraschino Cherries," "The Christening," "Villanelle for Thel," and "Booker Again"

Eleventh Muse: "Camille in America"

Feminist Studies: "Letter from Laura Cereta (Brescia, 1488)"

The Formalist: "Villanelle for Joe, on My Birthday"

Immortelles: Poems of Life and Death by New Southern Writers (ed. Thomas Bonner Jr. and Robert E. Skinner [New Orleans: Xavier University Press, 1995]): "The Bartender Reconsidered"

London Magazine: "Halloween on the Nile"

Louisiana Cultural Vistas: "On the Departure of My Guest" and "Moonrise on the Cane River"

Louisiana Literature: "Chess with My Mother"

The Louisiana Review: "After Reading Po Chü-i," "Egrets," and "Spider Lilies"

Maple Leaf Rag 15th Anniversary Anthology (ed. John Travis et al. [New Orleans: Portals Press, 1994]): "The Bartender's Hair"

Negative Capability: "Everything but Blue" and "Ode to the Big Muddy"

Piedmont Literary Review: "The Mermaid Story"

Prairie Smoke: The Pueblo Poetry Project, 1979–1989 (ed. Tony Moffeit [Pueblo, Colo.: Pueblo Poetry Project, 1990]): "The Maple Leaf Bar"

The Southern Review: "The Bottle Factory"

Tucumcari: "The Bartender's Tattoo" and "The Bear in Mid-life"

In memory of Helen Glynn "Honey" Kane (1910–2000)

Contents

1 New Orleans

This bar will be his mausoleum.
They're going to bury him in New Orleans.
  —Mike West, "Mausoleum"

Maraschino Cherries

Three little girls on the morning after,
out in the kitchen poking around
for cherries soaked in whiskey like a bomb
of grown-up secrets. Other times we found,

by Mom's clip earrings and kicked-off shoes,
blue glass monkeys on swizzle sticks,
doll-sized Oriental parasols,
cocktail napkins with jokes we didn't get.

Cherries as precious as Burmese rubies:
Once in a while, while the grown-ups slept,
we ate our fill of cherries from the jar,
but even then we liked the booze ones best.

The Christening

The only person in the christening room
who doesn't have a headache and bloodshot eyes
is the baby, wriggling like the neighbor's cat
we dressed in doll clothes, her mother and I,

when we were girls. Well, what the hell:
God made the Kanes for getting drunk.
Who knows the sad old Irish songs,
or loves the piano like flesh and blood,

except our family? Even the baby's
mother, as a child at dinner, dropped
her head on the table after too much wine,
giggling into the tablecloth.

Holding my very lively niece
over the stone baptismal font,
I feel like the thirteenth fairy godmother
hissing a prophecy no one wants

to hear: The priest will sign the cross
in oil between my godchild's eyes,
and Adam's sin will wash away,
but ours will wait like a harbor mine.

Kissing the Bartender

The summer we kissed across the bar,
I felt sixteen at thirty-six:
as if you were a movie star

I had a crush on from afar.
My chest was flat, my legs were sticks
the summer we kissed across the bar.

Balancing on the rail was hard.
Spilled beer made my elbows stick.
You could have been a movie star,

backlit, golden, lofting a jar
of juice or Bloody Mary mix
the summer we kissed across the bar.

Over the sink, the limes, as far
as you could lean, you leaned. I kissed
the movie screen, a movie star.

Drinks stayed empty. Ashtrays tarred.
The customers got mighty pissed
the summer we kissed across the bar.
Summer went by like a shooting star.

The Bartender's Clothes

I can't imagine you in winter clothes:
I think you were born for summer, I said.
You are no paper doll. You can't be folded

in and out of outfits tabbed at the shoulders,
even in my mind. You are yourself.
I can't imagine you in winter clothes.

I can't imagine your sunburst of gold
hair exploding on woolen lapels.
No Ken, no mannequin, you can't be folded

out of your beach-bright things that close
with snaps and strings, or slip overhead,
to be buttoned and zipped into winter clothes.

I can't imagine the air turning cold.
I can't imagine the daylilies dead.
And I can't imagine you in winter clothes,
tanned under wool like earth under snow.

Villanelle for Thel

The night he took me up against the wall,
the veins on his neck standing out like ropes,
I learned that life is not like books at all.

I was nineteen when I started to ball
politely with poets and bookish folk,
but in my thirties up against the wall,

bashing and banging like a poor rag doll
with a candy heart and no brains or bones.
I saw that life was not like books at all,

but more like headlines—barroom brawls,
a blues song sung with flatted notes—
the night he took me up against the wall.

Uncomprehending, my mother calls
my poems "vulgar" on the telephone.
She taught me how to read when I was small.
I tell her life is not like books at all.

The Bartender's Arms

Something unusual about his arms,
framed in a T-shirt with cutoff sleeves,
drew my attention behind the bar:

gold fuzz, baby fat, raised pink scars,
the rose tattoo in blue and green.
Something unusual about his arms.

Voices and asses and eyes had charmed
me previously, but arms? Good grief!
The way his shoulders drooped behind the bar,

as if he were a kitten in its mother's jaws,
front paws dangling, got to me.
Something unusual about his arms.

My own right mind and my upturned palm
warned me it would end in grief,
and still I leaned my elbows on the bar.

When I am eighty, wise, and calm,
and take this yellowed poem out to read
in liver-spotted hands and flabby arms,
I will be cured of men and bars.

The Bartender's Hair

Those nights I smelled a barroom in your hair,
I dreamed I saw you standing like a god
at closing time with Maddox huddled there

in the navy peacoat he used to wear,
thin as an X ray, pouring his Scotch
in a plastic cup, a barroom in his hair.

It was the change in the bedroom air
that woke me mornings at four o'clock
to find you lying beside me there,

rum fumes rising from your skin like a layer
of fog on the highway, and bar rags washed
in disinfectant in your barroom hair.

Where was Maddox? Sleeping on the stairs
of Mater Dolorosa, the Mother of Our Sorrows,
those nights I smelled a barroom in your hair,
the ghosts of cigars and perfume there.

Bar Noise

A blast of bar noise on the telephone.
Is the ceiling tin? Is the mural Fess?
He doesn't know where he is. I'm home.

So much for spending the night alone:
nightgowned, pimple-creamed, getting some rest;
the seven digits of my telephone

deep in his brain as breathing on his own.
Blanket to couch, I make a nest
to wait for him till he gets home.

On a bar napkin, in a hand unknown,
somebody copies my street address
from the chained book by the pay phone

to give the cab. He's a boomerang thrown
on the night's savanna, returning to the breast
that launched him. That's the doorbell, not the phone,
and it's his body, but nobody's home.

Halloween on the Nile

Off Luxor on a ship, I watched
the English waltz in stolen sheets
and tablecloths. You would have thought
a meeting of the Arab League
was taking place. No ice for drinks.
Date palms swayed along the shore.
My party favor, a camel doll,
leaked sawdust from its saddle sores.

Back at home it was afternoon.
My boyfriend would be getting up,
checking the mail for news of me,
pouring a shot in a coffee cup,
thinking about the costume ball
that evening, how his tennis shoes
would look with glitter on the toes.
Best go out for Elmer's Glue.

The loneliness we get at night
by water, with a rising moon,
can't be drowned in alcohol.
"Ah, Matthew Arnold, let's be true!"
I told the Valley of the Dead.
The tall Egyptian steward laughed
and kept on asking me to dance,
liking my pretty Irish mask.

Booker Again

Booker is dead, but I still go
sit on the Maple Leaf patio

among the palmettos and elephant ears
to listen to music and drink a few beers

and check on the pink hibiscus tree
firing its blossoms like flares at sea

late in the year. Mention his name
and the bar help repeats the same

handful of stories—how he vomited on
the keys one night and Big John

had to clean it up with a bar rag;
how the dope arrived by White Fleet Cab;

how he stood up once with his pantseat shitty.
Beauty is truth, but truth is not pretty.

The Bartender's Tattoo

I see men's arms and want a flower
carved into them, your rose tattoo.
I talk about it, eighty bucks an hour,
on days I try to be cured of you:
mentally peeling, burning, sanding
layers of cells as deep as it goes.
You were a walking artist's canvas.
You were a map with a compass rose.
You were the man who covered me
with roses fading red and pink
over my chest like a tapestry
tattooed in disappearing ink
every time I let you in.
The worst tattoos are under the skin.

Angel of Bars and Nightclubs

Angel of bars and nightclubs
Stick to him like a shadow
Thrown by a fishnet candle
Or a neon sign in a window

Lead him past the fighters
Cover his battered nose
With the feathers of one wingtip
Stick to him like smoke

Angel of pubs and taverns
Lead him past the bottles
Doubled along the mirror
Amber, topaz, emerald

Stick to him like music
And if his legs should falter
Swirl him into the folds of your robe
Past the boastful talkers

Angel of jazz and juke joints
Steer him past the women
Whose eyes go to the ear stud,
To the bulge, who do not love him

Stick to him like perfume
Guide him out the door
Past the marijuana smokers
Leaners on parked cars

Cups and straws in the gutter
Frat boys trying to puke
Angel of fallen angels
Angel of drunks and fools

The Bartender Quits Drinking

The Mater Dolorosa parking lot
is always full on Fridays during Lent.
I hear them chanting Stations of the Cross

as I double-park for the pastry shop,
this boozeless season giving us a bent
for doughnuts, candy, soda pop.

Twenty years ago, a schoolgirl, hot
in my coat, a lace mantilla on my head,
I swayed like them through Stations of the Cross,

thinking about forbidden choc-
olate ice cream, and dreading the dinner ahead:
fishsticks parceled out in meager lots.

Though I am not one of the good who got
a smudge of ashes to make amends
to Jesus for his time on the cross,

it's funny how the drinking stopped
to coincide with the start of Lent.
I mark each sober day with a cross.
I come to joy in a season of loss.

The Maple Leaf Bar

I wanted to understand the place:
the pressed tin ceiling and the out-of-tune
piano where the late James Booker played

in a rhinestone eyepatch and purple cape.
Bottles in sunlight like Arabian jewels:
I wanted to understand the place.

Maddox asleep like a cat onstage.
Kittens asleep in the storage room.
Red Sox, Celtics, and Bruins played

in bars that kept my uncles late.
They came home singing until they puked.
I wanted to understand the Saints.

What did you think, with your boyish face,
a bar rag tucked in your blue-jeans loop,
giving me all your change to play

the jukebox with? Another cra-
zy barfly making eyes at you?
I wanted to understand the place,
to play with words like Booker played.

Everything but Blue:

AFTER DIANE ACKERMAN, AND IN MEMORY OF
EVERETTE HAWTHORNE MADDOX (1944–89)

Although your eyes were everything but blue,
unable to digest the blue in light
(as most of us would turn away blue food,

not having eaten in a day or two);
although they were watery, rabbity, nearsighted,
farsighted, naked, and everything but blue,

it is by them that I remember you
the time of year blue china sells to brides
because there is no blue at all in food.

Ask any coroner: He'll swear it's true
our eyes turn greenish-brownish when we die,
just as a newborn baby's eyes are blue.

Your eyes were cinders when we carried you
to heave the ashes at the riverside
for greenish-brownish alligator food.

The river and the reeds were green-brown, too.
Above our heads, a February sky
absorbed white light but scattered back the blue
as you could keep down Scotch, but not our food.

The Bartender Reconsidered

If I were going to die a year from now,
would I take you back into my bed?—
rum on your breath, your body crashing down

thick as a tree after the furious pounding—
Thoughts that come from seeing the bald head
of a girlfriend dying a year from now.

No use digging a hole in the ground
here on the delta—the soil's too wet.
Displaced skeletons clatter down

on earlier bones above the ground,
clearing a shelf for the nouveau dead—
All of us dying years from now.

Girlfriends tell me to run you out of town,
some of them even with their dying breath.
Bones pile up and trees dig down.

Would I take you back for one more bout
if all my knowledgeable doctors said
that I was going to die a year from now?
What harm could come, when your body came down?

2 Baton Rouge

We used to drive
Thru Lafayette and Baton Rouge
in a yellow El Camino
Listening to Howlin Wolf . . .
He always said Louisiana
Was where he felt at home.

—Lucinda Williams, "Lake Charles"

The Mermaid Story

We've all heard half of the fairy tale:
A mermaid rescued a drowning prince,
swam him to shore, then pined away
because she missed the weight of him

and the heat of his breath against her neck;
nothing at all like the trickle of cool
saltwater flushed from delicate gills
when she kissed the mermen back in school.

But since there are witches underwater
as well as over, within a year
she'd bargained away her tail for legs—
and her tongue, too, as legs were dear.

She married the prince. His body hair
tickled like beachgrass parched in sun.
An eel grew where his legs forked.
(She couldn't speak this to anyone.)

2

Back in the antiuniverse,
a woman writer with two tongues
rooted to the floor of her mouth
like anemones has just swum

so deep with her freak tail,
the sea spins and her brain goes black.
We'll see if the tongue she bargained for
can send a message back.

Chess with My Mother

Maybe we'll get the chessboard out
when she comes home, and play again—
The tray stand wobbling over her sheeted
lap like mine when I was ten

and sick, too sick to lie on the couch
in the living room and watch TV.
I remember the concentration in
her face, bent over the printed sheet

of rules for hours. Across the room,
seahorses moved in a saltwater tank,
graceful in water, as if a pair of
knights had jumped their plastic stands.

In the beginning she always won:
I couldn't tell where the game left off.
Drifting in and out of my skin,
I heard her rattle the kitchen pots,

or thought I heard her gliding like
a queen across the checkered floor,
up the dark diagonals
of linoleum tile, and out the door

where Dad was coming home, one stately
sidewalk square at a time: our king.
Time went by. I tried my shaky
legs again, and started to win,

and she lost interest. Set up the board:
Here's a penny for the missing rook.
Here's a button for the missing pawn.
Pawns are children trying to be good:

They start out running, then catch themselves.
They never go past the end of the street.
Like all small children, they want to be hugged,
but love is what drops the queen.

The Bottle Factory

The summer after high school, seventeen,
I hired on at the bottle factory
in Nutley, New Jersey, to pack the lines
spun out by middle-aged Italian women
operating silk-screen machines. The work
was dumb: unfold a cardboard carton, place it
upright on a stand, insert a spacer,
pack a tier of tiny eyedrop bottles,
roof the bottles with a sheet of cardboard—
simple as layering lasagna noodles.
Each time a box was full, I'd heave it
off the stand, seal the flaps with masking tape,
start over—the only real excitement
coming from running too low on boxes,
wondering whether the boy would bring more
before my bottles toppled on the floor.

I liked to watch the women twirling up
blank bottles from the bin and wedging them
between two pins, which rolled the bottle surface
under the silk screen. Telling dirty jokes,
scratching themselves under cotton muumuus,
humming along to the theme from *Tommy*
(which came on right before the hourly news,
because the deejays could interrupt it),
they worked so fast their fingers were a blur.
Every so often a machine broke down,
and packer and operator had to scrub
defective bottles with acetone rags

until the maintenance man could fix it.
Nodding off to sleep from the acetone,
my rubber gloves as eaten through as cheese,
I drifted in and out of bottle dreams.

The day I turned eighteen, the legal age
to operate equipment in New Jersey,
the foreman put me on my own machine:
a slower model, off in a corner,
the size of a Chevrolet stood on end.
And so I turned out Wella Balsam bottles—
hair conditioner, brown and orange—
and sent them down my own conveyor belt,
humming along to the theme from *Tommy*.
I wasn't fast enough to need a packer
and, anyway, it wasn't automatic,
powered by foot pedal, moving when I moved,
a bashful, lummoxy dancing partner.
I learned to twirl each bottle for inspection,
to scrub a flyspeck from a dirty screen
with cotton rags wrung out in gasoline.

I wanted to be as fast as they were:
to break eight thousand, at least, like the slowest
worker, Dolores, who stamped gold leaf
onto April Showers talc. All day I raced
my best day's total, or her worst. Of course,
I wasn't Italian, or middle-aged;
I didn't live just outside of Newark
(still smoldering from last summer's riots);
by Labor Day I'd be off at college;
but I still longed to be good at something
physical: not words, but bottles.
I can't explain why it seemed important,
or why, for years after that, I cruised
strange drugstores looking for bottles I'd made
when love turned ugly, when words did not behave.

Camille in America

Back in the States for the first time since college,
Robert is trailed by an eight-year-old daughter
who speaks no English and shakes her head
when I offer her Coca Cola, water,

cookies, chips. Like Madeline,
the little French girl who stood in line
in a convent school in a children's book,
Camille knows patience. While her father drinks wine

in the living room, she sits at the kitchen
table drawing my cats in dresses,
word balloons coming out of their mouths.
Waving his arms, her father confesses

to flirting with countesses, lacking ambition,
cheating at tennis in Nice and Cannes.
"Papa, j'ai faim," she calls politely.
"Plus tard." I offer a peanut butter sand-

wich, tuna, ham: all unfamiliar.
Little black zigzag wags are sketched
around the tails of the cartoon cats
like danger around her father's head.

Later, we find a real French restaurant.
Robert orders her onion soup,
veal; but she only picks at the food,
follows me to the ladies room,

borrows my comb, then falls asleep
with her head down on the tablecloth.
Robert drinks brandy and smokes cigars.
Little gray curls of ashes drop

in his daughter's hair as he waves his arms.
Years from now, when Camille is grown,
she will say he looked like a movie star
the summer they crossed the sea alone.

Letter from Laura Cereta (Brescia, 1488)

I sit by my father's sickbed,
    wringing out cloths in cool water,

no more useful than my younger sisters,
    as he is too sick to be read to.

Tonight he waved away Homer,
    though I'd been hoping to practice my Greek;

later on a burst of hurdy-gurdy music
    floated up over the balcony from the street;

and I did not run out to gawk at them,
    the Neapolitan and his monkey,

but peered out from behind the draperies,
    as befitting a woman in mourning.

The monkey danced a jig
    dressed up in a man's cap and britches,

then swung up on a young girl's shoulder
    and kissed her on the cheek . . .

When I was that girl's age,
    my head was full of letters,

always cloistered in my father's study
    writing treatises in Latin—

Letter to Augustinus Aemilius,
        Curse against the Ornamentation of Women;

Letter to Bibulus Simpronius,
        Defense of Their Liberal Instruction—

How naïve I was, copying them out
        and sending them to scholars

as young men do,
        to establish their reputations!

Only one friar wrote back to me,
        though I gained some notoriety

here in my native Brescia—
        and then I was married.

The plague claimed my husband
        after eighteen months, no children;

I am glad to see that it spared
        the Neapolitan musician,

for what would the monkey do
        if his master were to die before him,

his head cold without a cap,
        and his legs twitching to music?

I busied myself for a while collecting
        a volume of my letters,

and published them six months ago,
        but no one has taken notice.

When my father dies my Greek will die too:
    it is not like Latin.

It fades from the mind so quickly,
    like a tune on the barrel organ.

The Bear in Mid-life

There are still nights she gets the bear:
fur gone, scarred with colored thread

from operations to stuff back stuffing
under ether from her chemistry set.

He's her age, but he's showing it:
cried in for spankings, moving vans,

goldfish floating belly up;
tossed around at summer camp;

posed on a hippie Indian spread
with blacklight posters, apple wine;

cried in another twenty years—
the major leagues of grief this time.

Who's to stop her, old as she is,
from taking the ratty thing to bed?—

needing the weight and shape of him
where her spent lovers dropped their heads.

Ode to the Big Muddy

1

Because I grew up a half hour's drive
from the North Atlantic, always within reach
of the dried-blood-colored cranberry bogs,
the ice bucket water, the desolate beach
with its circular rhythms, I looked down
on linear things, so like an erection
straining against a blue-jeans zipper,
always pushing in the same direction,
spine for brains. But I have learned to mimic,
quick for a girl, the river's predilection.

2

The first time I saw the Mississippi,
under the curving wing of a jet plane,
it lay there listless as a garden slug:
glistening, oozing, brown. Surely Mark Twain's
paddlewheel visions, Hart Crane's hosannas
to the Gulf, Muddy Waters's delta blues
hadn't sprung forth from a drainage canal?
"Fasten your seatbelts for descent into
New Orleans. Looking to the left, you'll see
the Mississippi River"—so it was true.

3

Unlike the ocean, the river's life is
right on the surface, bobbing there like turds:
a load of tourists on the *Delta Queen*
drunkenly singing half-remembered words
to showtunes played on steam calliope;
the push-boats nudging at oil tankers;
and nothing underneath but chicken necks
in crawfish nets, and our own dropped anchors.
The sea is our collective unconscious;
the river our blank slate, growing blanker.

4

And yet the river gathers memories:
the ugliest things grow numinous
over time—the trail of a garden slug
crystalline, opaline, luminous
when the garden slug itself has gone
as the river itself will one day go,
already trying to change its course—
an afternoon we watched the ferryboat
go back and forth until the sun went down,
skimming the water like a skipping stone.

5

Or the morning we gave back Everette's ashes:
homeless alcoholic poet-prince.
A cold March wind was ruffling the water.
Wouldn't you know, the ashes wouldn't sink;
so someone jumped in to wrestle them under.
It hit me then: I didn't want to die.
And so I made a choice, against my nature,
to throw my lot in with that moving line:
abstract, rational, conscious, sober—
cutting a path through human time.

3 St. Gabriel

The sunsets in St. Gabriel are fiery red
The fields all around are brown and dead
In St. Gabriel, St. Gabriel
   —Marcia Ball, "St. Gabriel"

Mapleworld; or,
Six Flags over the Maple Leaf

*So ye olde Maple Leaf has gone the way of all of the Cool. It
has been co-opted. Nothing escapes, because if you've heard of it
and it's not your usual, and you go there and you think it's cool,
others will follow, scribes will wax, poets will villanelle in the
washroom behind the bar, journalists will broadcast first in cool
papers and then real papers, then comes the new paint, micro-
brews, shitters sans orange algae, and no eau de crotch sweat,
only stuff with the name on it like vacationers' slides, but then
when the poets' minds go, it really is gone, and some other shit
becomes cool, but cool has changed. Who in Annapolis wants to
hear about how Tip's and the Maple Leaf "used to be"? Do we
want to hear about some "cool" Frisco haunt? No.*

   —M., via e-mail

You'd hardly recognize the Maple Leaf:
the bathrooms with their dim red Christmas bulbs
mercifully obscuring a half-inch-deep

primordial ooze, now eat-on-clean
for the Hard-Rock-T-shirt-clad mul-
titudes whose guidebooks canonize the Maple Leaf

the way it wasn't when we'd roll our jeans
to wade on in through the primeval flood
that covered up the heads a half-inch deep.

Dial soap dispensers and hot-air machines
are waging war on our *E. coli* bugs:
you'd hardly recognize the Maple Leaf.

Like shotgun shacks transformed to "galleries,"
our funky hovel has been gussied up
in Disneyesque façade a half-inch deep.

Who cares about the way things *used* to be,
except us creatures of the slime, who love
the darkness and the dead?—the Maple Leaf
with Booker playing, Maddox "just asleep."

Air and Angels on the Internet

1. Blindsight Villanelle

Suppose we don't need eyes for sight:
as Heraclitus pointed out,
the sleeper with his eyes shut tight

strikes a match to see at night
in dreams as in his waking hours,
which means we don't need eyes for sight.

Reaching for an object, blind
men curve their hands to fit around
its unseen contours, eyes shut tight.

If matter's only frozen light,
we're each a radiating cloud,
an aura sensed apart from sight.

Burglars, when they're televised,
have their features canceled out
by hovering swarms of pixelized

dots. That's what your face is like
in dreams, although don't ask me how
a person dreams of someone sight
unseen, or seen with eyes shut tight.

2. *Thoughtball Villanelle*

Suppose we don't need sound to talk—
suppose that nutcase Swedenborg
was right that angels banter not

in language but in balls of thought
wafting about like pollen spores
because they don't need sound to talk?

Think how in dreams our dialogue
flashes from mind to mind before
it's voiced, communicated not

in language, but its building blocks:
Chinese-poem metaphors
ideogrammed to the brain, not talked.

Who needs the *langue d'oeil* or *d'oc*
when we (like modern troubadours)
strum on lutelike keyboards not

quite sentences or finished thoughts
but runic clusters, bluesy chords
understood (though apart from talk)
like angel banter they can't be not.

3. *Chillbump Villanelle*

Suppose we don't need skin to feel,
since phantoms walking on our graves
can brush our flesh like something real

and punch it out in bumpy wheals
that take all afternoon to fade,
which proves we don't need skin to feel.

Incubi/succubi often steal
a screw when we're in alpha waves—
it feels so good, you'd swear it's real

(It made poor Saint Theresa kneel,
still tingling, by her bed, to praise
the Lord for what the married feel

a couple times a week. Big deal.).
Then there are those with amputat-
ed limbs who swear their pain is real.

Kindred souls on karmic wheels
beyond this plane, in hyperspace,
know what their astral bodies feel.
Who's to say that it isn't real?

4. *Tastebuds Villanelle*

What about taste without a tongue?
No need to stand there panic-stricken:
smell and not taste is what sparks hun-

ger pangs when stomach's full. Among
predaceans, bluff: "It tastes like chicken";
vegans, "squash." Who needs a tongue?

Stuck with four sounds, four colors, one
would opt for heroin addiction:
smell and not taste is what sparks hun-

ger pangs when all is said and done.
Patches of sweet/sour/salty/bitter
catch the four coin throws of the tongue.

Skin always tastes like salt and cum
like mushrooms, after all that friction:
smell and not taste is what sparks hun-

ger pangs. One might eat camel dung
gladly because of headcold-sickened
nostrils. Your off-limits tongue
tastes (a) like mint, or (b) like scum.

5. Brainstem Villanelle

But who can smell without a nose?
By that I don't mean who can *stink,*
but who can do what's done to rose

with that which (between Eskimos)
leads to all kinds of rinky-dink:
the carrotlike, snowmanic nose.

Think about how its vacuum hose
sucks up molecules of things
into the brainstem: dog turd, rose,

flecks of lover's skin—all goes
into the mind itself, commin-
gled there with thoughts about the nose.

Watch how I press his sticky-note
(scribbled in red Flair editor's ink)
up to my face like a written rose,

hoping it might dislodge one mote
of its creator's sweat or skin,
rocketing into brain and nose
thrilling as Yeats's or Dante's rose.

Ville Platte Villanelle

This is to inform you that I pissed
on the frozen soil of your hometown
Thanksgiving morning, and thank God I missed

my underpants and shoes and Silken Mist
L'Eggs panty hose, bunched up around
my ice-blue ankles as I pissed

on the landscape of your parents' tryst,
your first few steps—O hallowed ground,
now consecrated!—and thank God I missed

a pair of handcuffs on my wrists,
a turkey dinner in the Ville Platte pound
served up by deputies who might be pissed

I'd pissed and, therefore, by extension, dissed
the place that they were from, a one-foot-round
turf plug of it, now Agent Orange–crisped.

This is to inform you that you've kissed
a criminal. The rest rooms were shut down
Thanksgiving morning in Ville Platte. I pissed
on dirt as frozen as your heart, but missed.

Song for Ray

Sometimes another year goes by
One time the whole damn eighties
When I don't think of you at all
Your poetry and ladies

But lately I've been writing down my dreams, Ray
Lately I've been writing down my dreams

I might not recognize you now
You must be over fifty
That pretty Paul McCartney face
Vandalized by whiskey

Unless you sobered up inside some dream, Ray
'Cause lately I've been writing down my dreams

The way you dashed your poems off
At girlfriends' kitchen tables
Lesser talents famous now
Ray, you never saved them

Albas left behind beneath our toasters
While we still turned to hold you in a dream

I heard you gave up poetry
I heard you took up farming
I heard that you got married to
That girl who slept through parties

While dreaming that she'd get to take you home, Ray
To write about her breathing while she dreamed

I know that it's a bad idea
To resurrect a lover
There's been a change of attitude
They'll edit in a rubber

They'll make me be the woman of your dreams, Ray
I'm sleeping through this decade like a dream

Villanelle for Joe, on My Birthday

For once you're going to be like other guys,
not call me even though you said you'd call
to wish me happy birthday. My "surprise"

will be a silent phone and bloodshot eyes,
a soggy Kleenex wadded in a ball,
because you're going to be like other guys.

Beginning in July of eighty-five,
for all these years your reedy southern drawl
has wished me happy birthday—no surprise,

a sort of Northern Star to plot course by
through middle age, its map of losses, all
that makes us, once unique, like other guys.

An old pop record—*Judy's Turn to Cry?*—
that you, my fellow boomer, would recall,
expressed it: *What a birthday surprise!*

You'll stand me up and won't apologize
this year, old friend, but only by default.
You had to die to be like other guys,
your constant heart, time's loveliest surprise.

4 Natchitoches

Look in the water and see who is looking back
Does he look like someone you'd believe?
. . . I say all those promises are just reflections on the Cane.

—Joe Hardin, Rodney Harrington, and Jim Toney, "Reflections
on the Cane"

After Reading Po Chü-i

Like that old scholar-poet,
I've been posted to the far northwest to serve my state.
The only man in town who talks to me lives in his car
With a velvet tub chair and jars of peanut butter and jelly.
He says his ex-wife has money.
I have time to arrange my poetry books in alphabetical order.
In the mornings I sit out back longing to fluff the pink mating
      plumage
Cascading down the neck of a little blue heron,
And in the evenings I sit out back watching car lights flickering in
      the river,
Each fragile gold ingot a family returning from the cinema.
When my friend comes from the capital to visit me in his BMW,
His high-performance tires quivering on the brick streets of my
      village,
We do not raise a cup of wine to the quarter moon
Because this hard-won clarity has its own enchantment.

Egrets

You have to love them
for the way they make takeoff
look improbable:

jogging a few steps,
then heaving themselves like sacks
of nickels into

the air. Make them wear
mikes and they'd be grunting
like McEnroe lobbing

a Wimbledon serve.
Then there's the matter of their
feet, which don't retract

like landing gear nor
tuck up neatly as drumsticks
on a dinner bird,

but instead hang down
like a deb's size tens from
the hem of her gown.

Once launched, they don't so
much actively *fly* as *blow*
like paper napkins,

so that, seeing white
flare in a roadside ditch, you
think, *Trash or egret?*—

and chances are it's
not the great or snowy type,
nearly wiped out by

hat plume hunters in
the nineteenth century, but
a common cattle

egret, down from its
usual perch on a cow's
rump, where it stabs bugs.

Whoever named them
got it right, to be just one
r short of *regret.*

Spider Lilies

(ALSO CALLED "NAKED LADIES" IN NORTH
LOUISIANA, BECAUSE THEY PRODUCE NO
LEAVES UNTIL AFTER THEIR FLOWERS HAVE
BLOOMED AND WITHERED.)

After the first rain
in October, they spring up
in straight rows around

houses and grave plots;
something in their DNA
craves a human-drawn

line to follow, like
grade-school children writing their
names on a ruled page.

Up close, too, they look
more like kids' toys than like *real*
flowers: red plastic

pinwheels fastened to
green wooden sticks, with not one
wan leaf among them;

and in their centers,
where you'd expect to find sex-
ual organs and

sticky gold pollen,
is only nothingness, like
the crotch of a doll.

Yet when I go to
the poor Creole church at Isle
Brevelle this time of

autumn for their fair,
it's not the store-bought aster
nor the rich man's rose

that I find tucked in
the plaster folds of Mary's
dress with a child's hope.

My Window Tree

What was that flash of
green behind the window shade
in my guest bedroom?

Leaves, a whole tree branch
growing inside the house. Now
I understood why

all those beetles had
been sprinkled like sequins on
the ceiling and walls.

(It was no deathwatch.
No one had jeweled the roaches
like Huysmans's tortoise.)

Someone had smashed a
pane of glass to get in, I
guessed, but I was wrong:

nothing was broken.
The tree branch had tunneled in
using the channel

in the sash for the
string the window travels up
and down on. (As to

the beetles, they must
have entered sleeping in an
egg sac: they were too

big to march through that
pass, notwithstanding camels,
rich men, needles' eyes,

Jerusalem's hatch.)
Once through, the branch exploded
into leaves bright as

magicians' handker-
chiefs (no stuffing them back in-
to that narrow hat);

each leaf tilted its
solar dish up at the sun;
the beetle eggs hatched;

and for days I kept
dropping dishcloth or Bic pen
to pad back down the

hall for a peek, though
I knew in my heart the branch
would choke, the window

break, if I did not
prune the crippled growth I loved
dearer, Lord, than straight.

On the Departure of My Guest

I search my house late Sunday afternoon
making a list of what he's forgotten:
one travel-sized bottle of conditioning shampoo,
one breath mint at the end of its wrapper
surrounded by torn foil streamers
like a travel-sized spiral nebula.
Out back, by a pair of verdigris chairs
tilted to face the Cane River,
there's a cigarette stub in the dirt
still bearing the taste of mint,
and dangling from a cottonwood branch
is the pear-shaped hummingbird feeder
he left behind on purpose
to remind me of him with its red.
Because the birds don't trust it yet,
I walk to the edge of the river,
reach down the bank to pluck a trumpet flower,
and stick it in one of the holes
as he's nearing Opelousas.

War (Ants on the Hummingbird Feeder)

They won't cross a chalk line, he said, so—
Being a teacher and having a boxful on hand—
I stood on a lawn chair and daubed at the cottonwood's lowest
    branch
Until there was a white ring around it.
But the branch was three-dimensional, not flat like a sidewalk,
And the ants cut a double-lane Ho Chi Minh trail
Through knob mountains and peeling-bark lowlands
Where the chalk line had missed.

Ants, said my bird book, *can be stymied
In their attempts to take over a hummingbird feeder
By coating a section of the hanging wire
With petroleum jelly, mineral oil, or vegetable shortening—*
So I stood on the lawn chair again
Mounding fingerfuls of Vaseline
Onto the inch-long S-hook—
And it worked for a couple of days, just until
There were so many bodies piled up in the Vaseline bog
That the living were able to cross on the backs of the dead
The way the French crossed the trenches of Verdun.

Make the wire longer, said a voice—
Not that of the ants' angel—
So I unbent a coat hanger to its full length,
Buttered it with Vaseline, and stood on the lawn chair again
Hooking one end to the tree and the other to the feeder.
That did it. The ants surrendered
Just as the rubythroats were starting to leave town
For the orchards of Costa Rica,
Indifferent to the winner's cup
So many had lost their lives over.

Old Maid

Not fifty yet, in a long denim skirt,
I stand in front of my class taking roll.

Already my students aren't afraid of me,
Their preclass chatter like a waterfall.

Some days I'm afraid to write on the board:
There might be a spot of blood on my skirt.

Some days I'm afraid that the language I write in
Has slipped out of fashion like flat leather shoes.

Moonrise on the Cane River

The moon is a surprised white face over the darkening river
Even before a pair of blue-gray wings swoops down
Between the O of its mouth and the O of a surfacing fish,
And the phone rings, and it's you in Baton Rouge
Grilling a silver catfish and staring at the moon.

Illinois Poetry Series
Laurence Lieberman, Editor

To the Bone: New and Selected
Poems
Sydney Lea (1996)

Floating on Solitude
Dave Smith (3-volume reissue,
1996)

Bruised Paradise
Kevin Stein (1996)

Walt Whitman Bathing
David Wagoner (1996)

Rough Cut
Thomas Swiss (1997)

Paris
Jim Barnes (1997)

The Ways We Touch
Miller Williams (1997)

The Rooster Mask
Henry Hart (1998)

The Trouble-Making Finch
Len Roberts (1998)

Grazing
Ira Sadoff (1998)

Turn Thanks
Lorna Goodison (1999)

Traveling Light:
Collected and New Poems
David Wagoner (1999)

Some Jazz a While:
Collected Poems
Miller Williams (1999)

The Iron City
John Bensko (2000)

Songlines in Michaeltree: New and
Collected Poems
Michael S. Harper (2000)

Pursuit of a Wound
Sydney Lea (2000)

The Pebble: Old and New Poems
Mairi MacInnes (2000)

Chance Ransom
Kevin Stein (2000)

House of Poured-Out Waters
Jane Mead (2001)

The Silent Singer: New and
Selected Poems
Len Roberts (2001)

The Salt Hour
J. P. White (2001)

Guide to the Blue Tongue
Virgil Suárez (2002)

The House of Song
David Wagoner (2002)

X =
Stephen Berg (2002)

Arts of a Cold Sun
G. E. Murray (2003)

Barter
Ira Sadoff (2003)

The Hollow Log Lounge
R. T. Smith (2003)

National Poetry Series

Eroding Witness
Nathaniel Mackey (1985)
Selected by Michael S. Harper

Palladium
Alice Fulton (1986)
Selected by Mark Strand

Cities in Motion
Sylvia Moss (1987)
Selected by Derek Walcott

The Hand of God and a Few
Bright Flowers
William Olsen (1988)
Selected by David Wagoner

The Great Bird of Love
Paul Zimmer (1989)
Selected by William Stafford

Stubborn
Roland Flint (1990)
Selected by Dave Smith

The Surface
Laura Mullen (1991)
Selected by C. K. Williams

The Dig
Lynn Emanuel (1992)
Selected by Gerald Stern

My Alexandria
Mark Doty (1993)
Selected by Philip Levine

The High Road to Taos
Martin Edmunds (1994)
Selected by Donald Hall

Theater of Animals
Samn Stockwell (1995)
Selected by Louise Glück

The Broken World
Marcus Cafagña (1996)
Selected by Yusef Komunyakaa

Nine Skies
A. V. Christie (1997)
Selected by Sandra McPherson

Lost Wax
Heather Ramsdell (1998)
Selected by James Tate

So Often the Pitcher Goes to Water
until It Breaks
Rigoberto González (1999)
Selected by Ai

Renunciation
Corey Marks (2000)
Selected by Philip Levine

Manderley
Rebecca Wolff (2001)
Selected by Robert Pinsky

Theory of Devolution
David Groff (2002)
Selected by Mark Doty

Rhythm and Booze
Julie Kane (2003)
Selected by Maxine Kumin

Other Poetry Volumes

The University of Illinois Press
is a founding member of the
Association of American University Presses.

Composed in 10/13 Sabon
with Mural Script display
by Celia Shapland
for the University of Illinois Press
Designed by Paula Newcomb
Manufactured by Cushing-Malloy, Inc.

University of Illinois Press
1325 South Oak Street
Champaign, IL 61820-6903
www.press.uillinois.edu